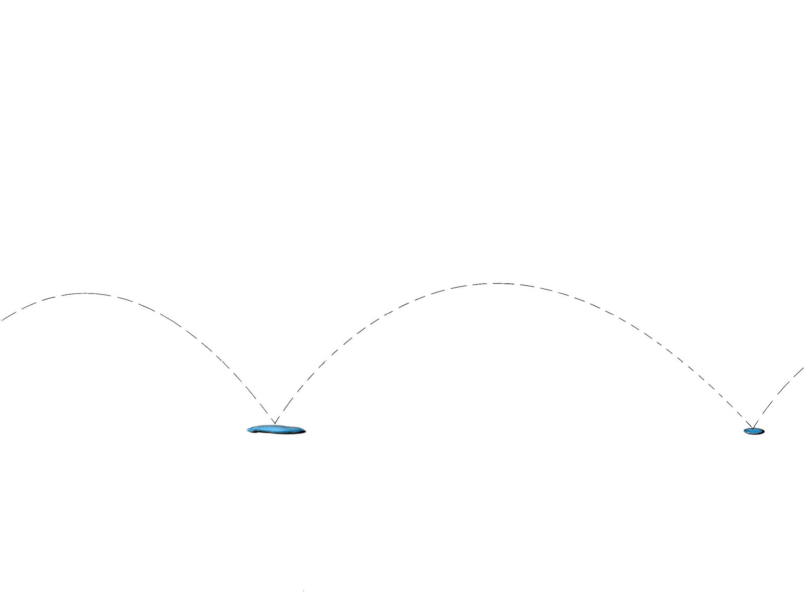

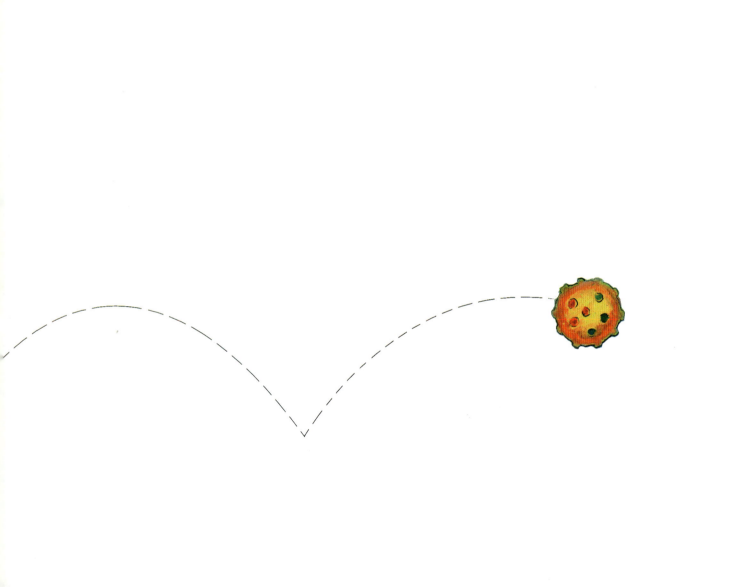

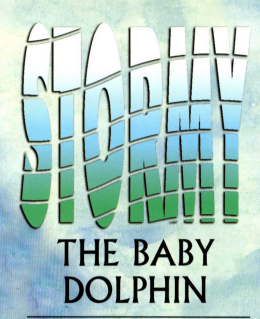

STORMY

THE BABY DOLPHIN

A Gulf Coast Rescue

Written by **Deb Adamson**

Illustrated by
Susan Schaub MacKay

EAKIN PRESS Austin, Texas

In recognition of the dedicated animal care staff and volunteers at Mystic Aquarium, the Texas Marine Mammal Stranding Network, and stranding networks throughout the world. This book is a tribute to your daily commitment and humane efforts to help save countless marine animals.

**A portion of the proceeds from this book will go
toward the care and feeding of Stormy.**

FIRST EDITION
Copyright © 2000
By Deb Adamson
Published in the United States of America
By Eakin Press
A Division of Sunbelt Media, Inc.
P.O. Drawer 90159 ☎ Austin, Texas 78709-0159
email: eakinpub@sig.net
▪ website: www.eakinpress.com ▪
ALL RIGHTS RESERVED.
1 2 3 4 5 6 7 8 9
1-57168-386-0

Library of Congress Cataloging-in-Publication Data

Adamson, Deb.
    Stormy the baby dolphin / by Deb Adamson.—1st ed.
        p.   cm.
    Summary: The story of a young dolphin separated from his mother during a tropical storm in the Gulf of Mexico, attacked by a shark, and then rescued by humans who eventually take him to the Mystic Aquarium in Connecticut.
    ISBN 1-57168-386-0
    1. Bottlenose dolphin—Juvenile literature. 2. Wildlife rescue—Juvenile literature. [1. Bottlenose dolphin. 2. Dolphins. 3. Wildlife rescue.].   I. Title
QL737.C432 A28 2000
599.53'0929—dc21   99-058124

To Craig for being the kind of love that dreams are made of.
To Mom for the gift of words.
And to Dad for the persistence to get things done.

—D.A.

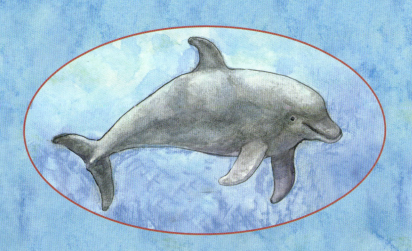

In the warm ocean waters just off the coast of Texas lived a mother Atlantic bottlenose dolphin and her **calf**. The baby dolphin would later be given the name Stormy.

Together they spent their days with a group of other dolphins searching the bright, clear water for fish to eat. Darting and diving deep, the mother taught Stormy how to surprise the fish from below. She showed him how to stun the fish with his **tail flukes**. And he learned how to locate them in the darkness with his special dolphin sonar skills. His mother even taught Stormy to follow along behind shrimp boats for free handouts from the fishermen.

All the while, the mother dolphin made certain Stormy remained close by her side. This kept him safe from danger, especially from hungry sharks.

One day Stormy and his mother were swimming with the other dolphins when the sun disappeared behind dark clouds. The wind began to blow. A tropical storm whirled across the ocean toward land. The waves swelled and angrily peaked in white, frothy swirls.

Stormy and his mother were tossed about when they came up above the water to breathe. Stormy tried hard to stay close to his mother. Listening carefully, he could hear her familiar clicks and whistles. He responded *click, click, click*, but it was no use. The sound was moving farther and farther away.

Stormy lifted his head up, **spy hopping** for his mother. But she was far from sight.

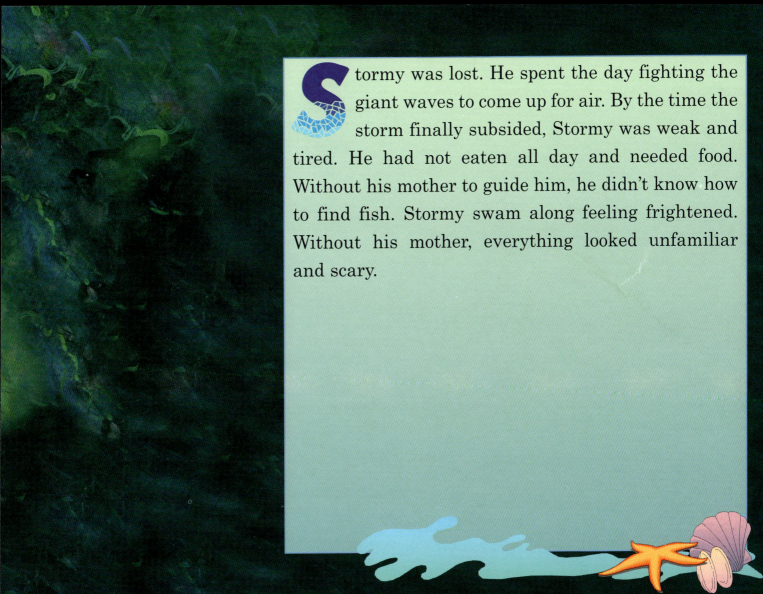

Stormy was lost. He spent the day fighting the giant waves to come up for air. By the time the storm finally subsided, Stormy was weak and tired. He had not eaten all day and needed food. Without his mother to guide him, he didn't know how to find fish. Stormy swam along feeling frightened. Without his mother, everything looked unfamiliar and scary.

Suddenly, out of nowhere, a shark spotted Stormy. A baby dolphin, weak with hunger, makes an easy meal for a shark. Stormy was attacked swiftly by the hungry shark. The first bite stunned him. But somehow Stormy found the energy to escape.

Stormy swam faster than he ever had before. The shark followed behind in the trail of blood. Faster and faster Stormy swam, not knowing where he was headed. Finally, the shark lost interest and swam away.

The baby dolphin was in pain. Stormy's **dorsal fin** was badly hurt. He also had a deep wound in his side. He was weak. He could barely lift himself up to the surface to breathe.

Several days passed and Stormy remained alone. He was unable to flap his tail to swim along. His small body was tossed helplessly in the ocean. The waves carried him to a sandy beach, where he lay scared and out of the water. Stormy was barely breathing.

Two people walking along the beach found Stormy. They called the Texas Marine Mammal Stranding Network for help. Volunteers soon arrived and placed Stormy in a special stretcher with openings for his flippers. They talked softly to him and wetted his sunburned skin with their hands. He clicked and whistled, calling out in the only way he knew how.

Stormy was driven by truck to the stranding center. A veterinarian tended to Stormy's wounds. Stormy was missing the top of his dorsal fin. He also had a large bite on his side. The veterinarian said it was a miracle that Stormy had survived the attack. Stormy thrashed a bit when the medicine was applied.

"Everything is going to be all right," the veterinarian said softly.

"*Phooof*," Stormy responded with a loud rush of air through his blowhole.

That night volunteers took turns holding Stormy up in the pool. He was gently lifted to the surface for air every few minutes. One of the volunteers, named Paige, sang gently until morning. It was Paige who gave Stormy his name. Stormy clicked and whistled until the sun came up.

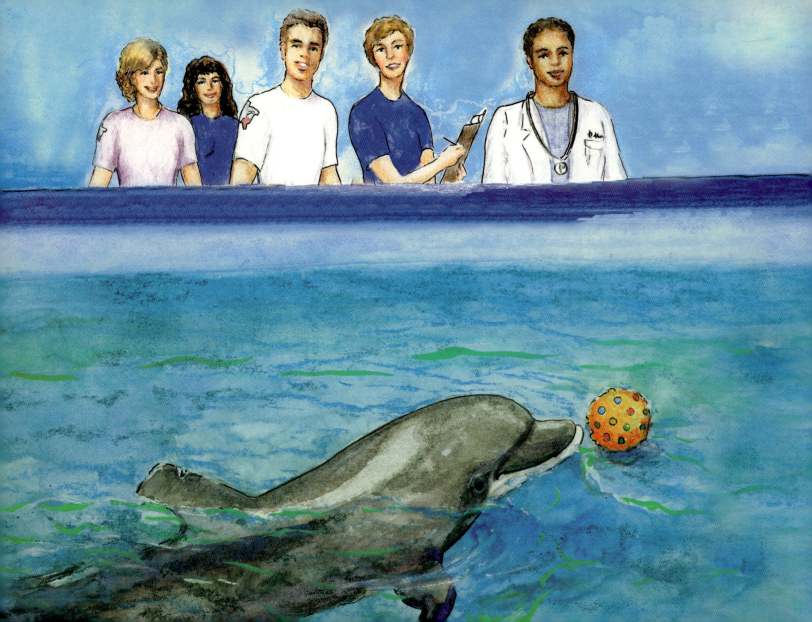

In the morning's light Paige fed Stormy mashed fish through a special feeding tube. The next day Stormy was offered whole fish, and he gulped it down. He swam for the first time without the help of the volunteers.

Day after day, Stormy grew stronger. His wounds were getting better. Stormy even got a special Internet web page so that anyone who wanted to see him could log on and follow his progress.

Still, he could not be released back into the wild. Stormy was only a baby and never learned all he needed from his mother in order to be safe in the ocean.

Finally, Stormy was taken off all medications. He was doing well. He even began to play with an orange ball tossed into his pool. The volunteers at the stranding center got ready to send him to his new aquarium home.

Scientists from Mystic Aquarium in Connecticut arrived to take Stormy with them. Stormy was placed back in his special stretcher and driven by truck to a nearby airplane. Stormy seemed worried. Paige came along so that he would feel more comfortable. She brought the orange ball.

During the flight, Paige sprinkled cool water over Stormy's back to help keep his skin wet. Stormy peeked through the stretcher, blinking his eyes and looking around.

When they arrived at Mystic Aquarium, Stormy was welcomed by schoolchildren with signs. Newspaper reporters and television crews lined the sidewalk.

The scientists took Stormy to a quiet area and gently lowered him into his new pool. The aquarium's two other dolphins clicked and whistled to Stormy. Stormy was shy at first, but then swam toward his new friends.

It had been months since Stormy had seen other dolphins. He flapped his tail flukes and swam closer to them.

Paige watched nervously. And then it happened. Stormy joined the others. They swam as a trio. It was as if Stormy remembered his days in the ocean exploring with his mother and the other dolphins.

Everyone cheered with delight!

Visitors came from near and far to see Stormy. They learned about him on the Internet and in the news. Most of them had never seen a dolphin up close before.

By visiting Stormy, people learn to appreciate the ocean as a home to many animals just like him. They learn that it is up to all of us to keep our oceans clean.

Of course, Stormy doesn't know he is teaching people these things. He is just happy. He playfully splashes and swims in his aquarium home, where he is safe.

Stormy at play—Mystic Aquarium.
—Photo courtesy Mystic Aquarium
/Steve Spencer

Afterword

This book is based on the true story of Stormy, the young dolphin separated from his mother during tropical storm Frances along the Gulf of Mexico in 1998. He was attacked by a shark, stranded, and then rescued by human friends who work with the Texas Marine Mammal Stranding Network.

Stormy's trip to the Mystic Aquarium in Connecticut received extensive national news coverage. People continue to flock to the aquarium, as well as watch live updates on Stormy via the Mystic Aquarium website (www. mysticaquarium.org).

Stormy continues to struggle for survival. At the time this book went to print Stormy began treatment for a serious bone infection believed to be caused by his shark attack. Veterinarians at Mystic Aquarium are hopeful that he will recover.

A happy life at Mystic Aquarium.
—Photo courtesy Mystic Aquarium
/Steve Spencer

Want to Know More About Dolphins?

★ Dolphins are not fish. They are mammals. Dolphins breathe air just like you and me. They don't breathe from their mouth. Air is taken in through the **blow hole** located on the top of the dolphin's head.

★ Baby dolphins are called **calfs**. They nurse on milk from their mothers for about two years. Mom teaches her calf everything he or she needs to know. After two years most dolphins leave their mothers and go off on their own.

★ Male Atlantic bottlenose dolphins weigh about 600 pounds when they are full grown!

★ Dolphins swim together in groups called **pods**. A pod can be made up of ten to one thousand dolphins.

★ Atlantic bottlenose dolphins can jump about twenty feet out of the water. It is the dolphins' **tail and flukes** that provide them with the power to jump so high.

★ The **pectoral flippers** are like arms to you and me. A dolphin uses pectoral flippers for steering and stopping in the water.

★ A **dorsal fin** is found on the dolphin's back. The dorsal fin helps a dolphin swim upright in the water. Stormy's dorsal fin was bitten by a shark, but he can still swim fine.

★ Some dolphins can hold their breath for up to thirty minutes, but usually they stay under water for less than a minute.

★ Dolphins can dive 1,000 feet below the surface of the ocean but usually dive to a few hundred feet.

★ Adult dolphins eat about thirty pounds of fish every day.

★ Dolphins are sometimes seen riding bow waves from boats in the ocean. Scientists think they are just having fun!

★ Dolphins sometimes follow fishing boats to catch any waste or bait fish being tossed overboard by fishermen.

★ Dolphins use **echolocation** to find food and objects under the ocean. Echolocation is like seeing with sound. Dolphins send sound waves toward a fish or an object. The sound bounces off the fish or object, returning information to the dolphin about the size, shape, and location. This is like sonar used in submarines.

★ The **melon** is the plump part of a dolphin's head. The dolphin's echolocation comes from inside the melon.

★ Dolphins **spy hop** to see above the water. They lift their upper body out of the water and look around.

★ Dolphins swallow their fish whole. They use their small, sharp teeth for grasping the fish—not chewing.

★ There are about thirty different species of dolphins found throughout the world's oceans. Stormy is an Atlantic bottlenose dolphin. **Atlantic bottlenose dolphins** are found in the Atlantic Ocean and the Gulf of Mexico.

★ Dolphins whistle, squeak, pop, and chatter. They use all these sounds to communicate with each other. **Signature whistles** are the sounds that individual animals make. Scientists think this is how dolphins know one another.

★ Dolphins don't sleep like you and me. They are always on the alert for **predators**, like a hungry shark. So, instead of closing their eyes and being in the dark, they swim slowly at the surface of the water, resting lightly and breathing.

What You Can Do For Dolphins

Learn more about dolphins in any way you can. Understand what is happening to them in the wild. The more you know, the more you can do to help save them if they are in trouble from overfishing, hunting, or pollution.

Visit aquariums and zoos that have dolphins. Ask questions and listen carefully to staff. There is always something new being learned and shared.

Eat dolphin-safe tuna. This tuna is caught in a special way so that it keeps dolphins safe from possible drowning in fishing nets.

Never feed wild dolphins if you see them in the ocean. They eat a special diet and should not become dependent on people for food.

Don't try to pet a wild dolphin. They could bite!

If you see a dolphin that needs help, contact the local police or a stranding center near you. There are specially trained people who know exactly what to do for a sick or injured dolphin.

Keep our oceans clean by throwing trash away in the proper place, recycling, and participating in beach clean-up efforts in your area.

Deb Adamson is the public relations director for Mystic Aquarium in Mystic, Connecticut, where it is her job to inform the public about dolphins like Stormy, and a variety of other marine life. Her love of animals is what inspired her to write Stormy's story. This is Adamson's second book for children. She wrote the rhyme for *Monkey See Monkey Do: An Animal Exercise Book For You!*, which features a menagerie of critters that encourage children to mimic animal movement. Adamson lives on the shoreline of Connecticut with her husband Craig and one grumpy old cat.

Susan Schaub MacKay spent her childhood in Mystic, where she made countless visits to the Mystic Aquarium. Classically trained as a portrait painter and sculptor, she has a passion for painting animals. She also plays keyboards in an original, traditional country band. She and her husband Chris share their home with four beautiful cats.